Manifest.oh!

*a manifesto for peace
and convivial living*

Andrew Geoffrey Kwabena Moss

First Published: 2023

10 9 8 7 6 5 4 3 2 1

ISBN 978-0-6454326-5-7

Printed & Bound in Australia

Published by RoseyRavelston Books

roseyravelstonbooks.com

I – Race & Migration

Wake Up Call
Melanin Masked White
Misread
Mature Cheddar Gorging
Liverpool Eight Names
Saintly Francis
Storm Brewing, a New Dawn
Nyankopoxyican Breath of Fresh Air

II – Housing

The Fire Last Time
Concrete Griots
Housing Hate Inflames
Songs of Grime
The Schoolboy Trap

III – War

War Crimes
Union straitJacket
Empire 'Free'style
Another World's War
Copy & Paste
Chant Down Marble Men
(Un)Reachable Moments

IV – Peace

Crusades
Ordinary Hybrid Bliss
Smethwick Melts
Fly a New Flag

I

Race
&
Migration

Wake Up Call

'Post' racial racisms proliferate at the wake
Maggots burrow and suck the marrow
Of the bony body, stiff, upper lipped, quivering
Where supposedly race has died
Rigor Mortis
Rigorous post-mortem sets in

We sit in its wake, denying the corpse
Unvoiced
Brutalized by the ghost – invisible institutions
Structured denial, structures of the mind
Post-mortem staining
Livor Mortis blue, veins deoxygenated, bruised
Trodden down, choked by the boys in the same hue
And cry the threats
Quelled, securitized
surveillance capital capturing insurgents
by militarized law forcers
caught on the grainy black and white reality CCTV
Animalized in Gazan strip search malls,
Mauled beside Ferguson's suburban stores
Contained in a wooden box, bodies bagged
Body's race declassified in the state morgue
A race to legally deny
Neo-liberal accountability privatised
Outbreaks, viralities, skirmishes informalized
Penetrating gated communities and nations

Murmurs on the 'Make Britain Great Again' News
Channelling emotional narratives
Irrational unevidenced indignation

Speakers spit and hiss poisonous noises
Surround soundbites of disavowal
Anti-Woke Culture Wars waged against a home front
truth
National Service rings in ears, called to action
Death knells toll, entrenched
Hollow sounds in post-truth age battles
History rewritten, weaponised,
Perpetrators victimised

Unearthed historical facts, developments arrested; held
hostage
by eulogized mythologies, emotional narratives
Covered up, unevidenced indignation,
Electronic pages rewritten and shared from ivory towers,
White Houses, Parliaments of snowy owls defecating,
disseminating
Bubo scandiacus, scandalous excretions
Fake acidic news, dropping ammonia pellet bombs of
undigested truths
From rooves, whilst beneath them
the undocumented polish whitewashed glass ceilings
Ethnic cleansing, ethical cleaning

Wiping down the blood splattered walls
Entranced halls of un*stately* homes, historic edifices
Systems, structures built on the foundations
Of a disappearing, Bermudian triangle of transatlantic
slavery
Baroque gold gilded framed portraits
Vanishing points of reference, reverence

Country houses for those seeking asylum
Amputees immobilised, shell-shocked cultured
Victims, entrenched survivors of colonial empires
Sit then sleep in a post-Brexit divided, ruled,

Above the eye, identity clings to soils
Ploughed embattled furrowed brows
Born and raised rich, dormant garden beds of privilege
Signalling denial

Hedgerow colonial countryside, gangrene unpleasant land
Suffering the blight of a Black Plague, bubonic, ruins
The bucolic myth of Merrie England reimagined
Rebuilding Hadrian's Walls, Fortress Britannia barricaded
Arcadia manipulated with Capability the Browns and
Blacks and Others
Banished from the Middle of English villages
Subjects to anthroporacial fertilisation,
pesticides and sterilisation, vanish
In a court of disapproval, donned, undone, unacademic:
A squad of climate scientists and historians of Empire
Lined up and sentenced by jesters: jingoistic juries jeering
Cheered on by structures of denial and disapproval
Denounced unpatriotic leftie liars.

Rigorous post-mortem sets in
Rigor Mortis
Where supposedly race has died
On the bony body, stiff, upper lipped, quivering
Maggots burrow and suck the marrow
'Post' racial racisms proliferate at the wake.

Melanin Masked White

White masked melanin
Avatars of illusion
Lightening the dark from within

Black souls constructed by white folk
Doubly conscious, born with the caul of second sight
Constricted complex-ions
Tightened tensions
Colonially manufactured neuroses

In a laboratory lined by test tubes, tied in delirium
Incoherent, de-negrification serums
Disguising appearances, de-blackening histories
Skin bleaching agents causing irritation
Ochronosis, blue-black discolouration and disease
Mercurial poisoning of pores
No pause for thought

Squeeze the pipette of pigmentocracy
With one drop of hypocrisy
Into the petri dish of dreams
Create pigments of the imagination

Commercial cosmetics of whitewashing
Noxious concoctions to conceal blemishes
Colour privileges, avatar of Western prejudice

Melanin white masked
Avatars of illusion
Darkening the light.

Misread

This poem is dedicated the lost civilisations and nations, the dispossessed and misplaced, judged and re-covered, pages flicked through and cast aside on dusty bookshelves.

Dear Reader, where should I begin?
As I flick through the pages within,
Far from the back where the chapters are fat?
At the back pages where they're faded and withered,
Mottled, dog-eared and torn with a jaded tinge?
Or in the lean lithe middle, past the pages that giggle,
Before complications twisted plots?

You have an exotic cover
Bound to be published by private press
The blurb speaks of persuasive eccentricity
British brogue, Ghanaian ancestry
History's pages have stolen and enslaved us
Historiographies and Holocausts
Stamped in the past,
Now I'm scanned by a red glow of fear
Uncertainty classified between
Afro-futuristic fiction and postcolonial non-fiction
Liminal post-Dewey systems

The illustrations disappointing
Only drawn in black and white
Ill-fitting fictions
Roughly sketched depictions
Of seldom heard voices

Proofread too many times for sin tax
My cohesion is intact
Across paragraphs and Trans-Atlantic pages
I bounce forth and back
A polysemic text
Vexed by an old-fashioned reading.

Mature Cheddar Gorging

'You black people!' Eva the optician quipped
    with a sardonic straight face and stiff upper lip
    high on white wine, a post-racial mischief of our times,
    a drink mixed with flirtation and fear in equal parts
at a dinner party of classy white privilege,
somewhere in deepest darkest Somerset, not far from
Wells
Offering the cheese platter, to Hakim the lecturer,
it was time to make a statement

Cured meats, salami, prosciutto, olives and crackers,
what a feast! 'Umm…' Hakim eyed up the exotic cheese on
offer,
there were so many options on the platter:
   aged: gouda, gruyere; soft and creamy: epoisses, burrota,
    the freshest mozzarella; crumbly: goat and feta
     a smoked selection: gouda or provolone?
       Or was he lonely, feeling blue enough: for
Roquefort or gorgonzola?

'Something straightforward,' he picked up the Red Leicester
   caressing it on to his cracker, the next selection he lifted
up
     the cheddar, like a gemologist, with lapidary
hesitation, assessing treasure

Hakim held it up for introspection, an encrusted sliver
of off-white gold rectangular cheddar
'This reminds me of a gem, a horrific hidden history!' he
beamed
Evidently all was not quite what it seemed, smiling at his
interlocutor

Eva flapped her eyelids and curtseyed, weak at the knees
'A discovery… made no less, on the edge of this very village,
it's best to support local industry…'
'You speak in riddles.'
'Then I'll continue. Remember it was in all the papers
The skeletal remains discovered in the caves,
        not far from here, in Cheddar Gorge.'

Eva nodded in encouragement
  'It was ground-breaking what they unearthed!
    The Mesolithic skeleton in the British wardrobe,'
Laughing at the pun let out of the closet, Eva nodded on
    'Cheddar Man, the oldest of us Homo Sapiens, quite the
man!'
'DNA analysis by modern-day trepanning
The scientists drilled a two-millimetre diameter hole,
extracting a few milligrams of powder from the bone
A toothless wonder so no enamel oxygen isotope
'Eva, d'you know why they did it?'
She shook her head in disbelief
'Drrr…'he teased and mimed a dentist drilling
 '….to get the full genome!'

'Then next-gen shotgun sequencing, defining myriad DNA
random fragments across the genome
They created a database and mapped his against the DNA
of modern human genomes, you and I.'

'Cheddar Man, the forensics suggest, left Africa
and headed to the Middle East, then west to Europe
our neighbour, he crossed Doggerland.' Eva frowned
'The ancient land bridge,' came the explanation
Again, she flapped her eyelids 'The old Eurotunnel…'
Isn't he funny she thought, thoroughly smitten
'…that connected continental Europe to Britain,'
His good looks caused distraction

'the original refugee identity crisis you might say!'
'Get ready for the twist,'
   Licking his lips, pausing before
      he crunched the Cheddar cracker
gripped in the vice of his thumb and forefinger

'Guess what it looked like…'
  'I'm not sure,' Eva responded, 'pale skin, fair hair, like *me*
of course.'
'Sorry to disappoint the pigments of your imagination.
Brits developed pale skin much later…'
'Do go on,' pressed Eva, dressed in shock

'CHEDDAR MAN WAS **BLACK**!'
Hakim announced in bold capitals
The dinner party's heart attacked,
The clinking of champagne flutes
Stopped
 Frozen
  In deafening Silence
'He had blue eyes and dark to black skin!' he uttered
triumphantly
'Today Eva, ten per cent of British ancestry can be linked,
they think, to this ancient population
That means about twelve of you here, besides me of
course!'
Hakim staged a guffaw,
spinning   around and bowing
spectacular showman, theatrically at his audience

'*You're* the *optician* Eva, here's one in your eye
"You black people!"
The Cheddar Superiority Complex put to the test!
We black people, earlier, didn't you mean?'

Liverpool *Eight* Names

Liverpool 8 names, playing out racist games
in a stadium of hate, under the floodlights
that lost their *shine*, instantly dimmed dark
A Polaroid faded light over time, photoshopped, gentrified
Gladiators deflecting heat with thick skinned shields
radiating from chariots of fire
whether in Anfield or Goodison Park
modern colosseums feeding Africans to lions
Puzzle People torn and left to pick up the pieces

Negro in the forties, *Mixed Race* sixties *Shines*
Coloured a *half-caste* in the nineteen seventies
Afro-Caribbean eighties status, *Ethnic Minority* nineties
Ticking a box, somewhere on a millennium
Ethnic Monitoring Form penned stateless

The sixties shines darkened by Scouse black humour
Half cast aside, half apart from Fathers without Mersey phrasebooks
who clung to the last pages of yellowing institutions:
The Federation, The Crew Club, The Sierra Leone,
The Nigerian, The Yoruba, The Ethiopian, The Ibo
Dreaming of setting sail on fresh zephyrs to Africa again
No reason why their sons and daughters could not assimilate
Docked from slavery, colonialism, poverty and wars
Trying to shield their children from racial tortures and slurs

Born in Liverpool lonely, home not a free town Sierra Leone
Here to stay but isolated as a *Yellow Man, Half Breed, Red*

Confronted in streets head-to-head, considered English
by their Fathers, born in the middle of an ocean, lost
in a Bermudian triangle of transatlantic slavery
Feet in all camps: Africa, language, Liverpudlian culture
Carrying on a revolt, brave, continuing lineage of diaspora
slaves
Be it in Massa's plantation/ targets of the KKK/ rioters in
Watts
Apartheid Soweto home townships/ Ashanti warrior war
fields
Maroons in Jamaican mountains/ Mau Mau resisting
Painting Washington BLM yellow/ part of a proud Nation

Games of classification, nominated nomenclature
Pencilling fifty shades of degra(y)dation
Shards of glass pressed into hearts deflating
Darkie, glasses worn to avoid the experience of *Shines*
Lenses framing innocence 'No 'arm was ever meant, soft
lad.'

'You'll Never Walk Alone' the chant
for Barnes bananas thrown and monkey groans apart
Bananas split, both sides in laughter
Aping civilisation terraces of institutionalised racism
Cheered on in the stadium of hate, Jekyll and Hyde
Whilst they applaud the Caucasian scorers
without pause or falter, haitus from terrace torture
Walking through a storm, head held high, unafraid of dark

Wandering across from Red to Blue
Through an A-Z maze of slaver street names
past Penny Lane, it drops, James Penny
Strawberry Fields of blood run bittersweet
Wrapped in cotton wool Protectionism at all costs
to stem against the Union flow, the *Oreto* leaves, in secrecy,
Enrica renamed *CSS Alabama*, supporting Confederacy

Capturing, burning and sinking sixty-five merchant ships
Arriving at Everton's proposed new home
Bramley Moore's Docksite Stadium to Slavery
Slaveowner and merchant of Brazilians
Complicit in the violence of middle passage misery
Financing clandestine voyages, lucrative deliveries
Who spoke out against an Act in Parliament
against British naval ships inspecting for enslaved cargoes
Receiving Pedro II's Order of the Rose

Liverpool 8 names, playing out racist games
in a stadium of hate, under the floodlights
that lost their *shine*, instantly dimmed dark
A Polaroid faded light over time, photoshopped, gentrified
Gladiators deflecting heat with thick skinned shields
radiating from chariots of fire
whether in Anfield or Goodison Park
modern colosseums feeding Africans to lions
Puzzle People torn and left to pick up the pieces

Negro in the forties, *Mixed Race* sixties *Shines*
Coloured a *half-caste* in the nineteen seventies
Afro-Caribbean eighties status, *Ethnic Minority* nineties
Ticking a box, somewhere on a millennium
Ethnic Monitoring Form cutting costs

Carrying on a revolt, brave, continuing lineage of diaspora
slaves
Be it in Massa's plantation/ targets of the KKK/ rioters in
Watts
Apartheid Soweto home townships/ Ashanti warrior war
fields
Maroons in Jamaican mountains/ Mau Mau resisting
Painting Washington BLM yellow/ part of a proud Nation
Walk on, walk on with hope in our hearts

At the end of the storm there's a rainbow
and a sweet golden song of calypso
We will never walk alone. This is our home.

Saintly Francis

Francis sweeps the floors in hope
Soaps down dirty walls
Knocks, gingerly
at the Headteacher's emerald door
before he vacuums her red-carpet floor

His life in a vacuum of another
Type, he waits for his papers
from the Home Office
Whilst we paper over the cracks
of the injustice
saying prayers behind his back

Francis, an accountant by trade
Counting down his days
Waiting for his papers
Abacus beads of perspiration
Sweat glistens, drip
I listen in to his tragedy
He explains his narrative in optimistic lilt
Lullabies of Sierra Leoneon Krio
Tones tinged with French accents
Where r's and w's collide
Waiting for his far from Home Office papers
Paper chained delays
He's a number, numbering
the days,
made Stranger
numbed by delays
Waiting for a stamp
Approval at a cost.

Storm Brewing, a New Dawn

For inky warriors everywhere, ink dem

Did you see the weather forecast, the barometer of our
times?
Watch the storm in Norbury and Thorton Heath arise?
It's creeping far beyond, betwixt between beneath
Reach seismic wavy tentacles, carving earth asunder our
feet
It's recorded daily on smartphone metronomes
As we breathe our lyrical beats into electronic, obsidian
tomes
receivers. Dictate to Blackberries in 16 bars of hope
Griots like Stormzy stir cauldrons, viscous in mischief

Within the bubbling multicultural crucible
froths disbelief, cotch in Croydon council flats
raise up our fists, grip pens and mics, attack,
stirring against Atlantic tides, our liquid boils resistance
the salty whips and chains of history lashed upon our skin
instead, we engrave a forever legacy, longer lasting
On the mic we rise, and on the page, they turn

Jumping out of pens into inky fountains,
In puddles, we spurn in murky indigo
Capoeira gyroscopes orbiting two worlds-
connect the misty heavens and fiery depths of hell
we rage, indigenous survivors, spit Maori tattooed tongues
dance our dark battles on canvases of caramel

Anansi's carapace parachute emerges in the swell,
looming in jungle concrete towers,
from bullet proof invested Union strait Jack-ets, it shoots
and spins, weaving silky kente signatures
in adinkra symbolism,
abseil graffitied city walls, unleash
threads pulled out from hind legs like knives,
Through spinneret spigot nozzles, inner liquid
turns to silk, the gossamer strings,
umbilical cords that sing
and DNA dance, double helix genetic memory
in and out of ropes,
beyond those grimy walls and stairwells urine soaked,
In Thorton Heath and Norbury, watch them rise up with
dread
Voices conquering the storm, climbing up the web
Pull super-tensile strings, baton down the hatches,
Navigate greasy poles, connect across diaspora,
Behold break open the ceiling glass,
a new dawn is arising, we must seize the chance.

Nyankopoxyican Breath of Fresh Air

'We can't breathe!'
cried the diasporic seeds on barren soils
Signals sent by those tethered
to Africa, Europe and the Americas
Inhospitable stormy weather
Picked up on marine radar radio
by Deep Sea Drexciyan Dwellers
Riding high under waves of isolation
In a Bubbled Metropolis
Travelling on Aquabahn in Cruiser Control

'We can't breathe!'
Weak breath signals picked up
In Africa, Europe and the Americas
Inhospitable stormy weather

Progeny of those labelled sick and disruptive
Thrown off foul scented slave ships
on their Middle Passages
They swam from their mothers' wombs, learning to
breathe
to found subaqueous empires and freshwater trajectories
Formed deep seated civilisations beneath
a vast dark abyss
created by transatlantic slavery
Brave, alternative histories

'We can't breathe!'
Weak breath signals picked up
In Africa, Europe and the Americas
Inhospitable stormy weather

Valiantly escaping through aqua worm holes
Enslaved removals evolved into wave-jumpers,
stingray and barracuda battalions
to Positron Island, Bubble Metropolis, Danger Bay
Reaching Drexciya in stages
Evolutionary deep Black Atlantic Ocean navigation
An aquazone surrounding isolated archipelago

'We can't breathe!'
Weak breath signals picked up
In Africa, Europe and the Americas
Inhospitable stormy weather

The next Drexciyan Quest:
Communicate to save land lumbered souls
from the prison industrial complex, colonisation,
decolonisation, institutional racism, post industrialisation,
macro and micro-aggressions,
global warming oppression

'We can't breathe!'
Weak breath signals picked up
In Africa, Europe and the Americas
Inhospitable stormy weather

They sent sonic invasions
From their underwater techno-pirate-stations
Helping those struggling to survive
Adverse, intense climatic changes
Attacking the mainstream of airwaves
Allowing oppressed souls to breathe

A rescue mission dreamt up by Drexciyan R.E.S.T
Research, Experimentation, Science and Technology
New systems to allow breathing were developed

In the tropos-, stratos-, mesos-, thermos-
and eventually exospheres
Finally, flying, releasing estranged cousins,
from the effects of transatlantic slavery
Breathing

'We *can breathe!*'
In deep sea and space

Terrestrial, seabed to exospheric adaptation
Travelling dimensional portals,
jumping-holes at liminal crossroads
Neo-evolution from Drexciyan to Nyankopoxican
Extra-terrestrial storm weathering then harnessing

Formation of a single, continuous superfield
Hybrid reality, mediating all mass, space, time and energy
Innovative Molecular Enhancement Technologies
The stolen plotting liberation after surviving
abject global conditioning
Deep in the ocean, on land and air

Soul survivors, regrouping,
readying for the Journey Home (Future)
Wherever we choose to go.

II

Housing

The Fire Last Time

The fire last time, burned
without sympathy, a New Cross tragedy
stoked by Powell's red blood fuel
Crucified by race hate, five weeks too late

A letter to Sybil, addressed to 'her' people
No tea or biscuits or sympathy from the PM
or Queen, nothing to the families bereaving
Yet Thatcher sent condolences to a Dublin club
that went up in smoke, some kind of sick joke

Set apart from true blue Brits, who pull up
a chair and sip, feet comfortably under the table
Allowed to work and live, in cold shouldered Britain
whilst victims are labelled hot headed criminals

Fuel to the anger in fiery aftermath
of smoke screened insults, devices incendiary
Tongues of flame silencing a youths' birthday party
Thirteen dead and the perpetrators unsentenced
An unpunctuated army turn their backs,
Harassing loud black house parties

Police vigilante mobs stop and search
For black culprits, spreading disinformation
Framing and forcing false conclusions, confessions
Party goers and families under the spotlight
of intense interrogation
pressure builds to sign a statement

There had been a fight before the flames,
took hold, the fuselage of a firebomb theory implodes

Thatcher's secret police dismantle a welfare state
stoking embers of working-class hate
marked by the spray can of Deptford's NF
poison penned letters, delivered by brick

Across town in Fleet Street, papers underplay racist attack
Reports filed, disorderly West Indian behaviour,
criminal records of reprobates, neighbourly judgements
add insult to the burning destruction, a cover up

Thirteen dead and nothing said,
Come what may we are here, past, present, future
To stay in the heat of a 1981 inferno
439 New Cross Road, a raw flesh wound
Inflamed, infects the street's veins
Civil riots explode, on the ashes of grief
molotovs explode, rise up like Phoenix.

Concrete Griots

Concrete griots taught
to suck and grit grilled self-defensive ivories
their tusks and mothers' tongues ripped
out by colonial expeditions
Baring then in grimy bedsits next to penthouses
in the subterranean city's underbelly
bowels, the white noise of flapping jowls and cheek of it

Turn the other cheek,
lift up your chipped shoulders
we are told! This our inheritance, our gift
from ancient ancestral homes of gold,
chief's orchestras and linguists' staffs
Now whipped into action
Stem the blood and bandage it
In Nubian pyramids, sarcophagi
embalm our elemental spirit

As we make our way up and down tower blocks
celotex insulates middle classes
in gentrification, so their views stay intact
whilst toxic plastic clad combustibles
catch light, and crumble ash to ash
stick in the stairwells of tears in eyes
elevators no longer lift
The broken-down blotted out
Streets in the sky sob hooded raindrops,

Cotch and break bread in Blake Tower
toasting songs lost, of innocence, experience
In bleak Dickension workhouses of grief

Paint peels to Bow bells and jellied eels
preserve injustice in aspic
Peeling Terry's Clockwork Orange chocolate-
ticking time bombs in Thamesmead
Stony islanders hewn at the cutting edge
of concrete rectangular prisms, trapped
strapped for cash, in hands gripped
with fatigue, balaclava and baseball bats
Over-cast leaden firmament
We traipse, modern zombies,
over sleeping policemen
obstacles on the pavements of enslaved
estates of new world bitumen plantation

Held in the shank of shackles,
chain-gang sign laws executing turf wars
and postcode lotteries, Molotov cocktails
knocked back, Black Russian roulettes spin
While we fed in cages, thrown banana skins
caught slipping in a system, trapped
Racist abuse hurled and chanted us

Sound-clashes with Babylon systems of authority
Dub plates of treasure spat
And turn the tables in pirate stations
under constant surveillance
in states, boroughs and counties of hateful racism
Fallen victims stabbed, gunned up and down,
languishing against boarded up shopping parades
and coin launderettes of money,
        slotted in the tower blocks
of anti-social housing out of eye shot
peppered pinholes of bullet spray
Youngers on rusty BMXs and mopeds
Up and down roads and county lines
swallow rocks and wash down hopes

slim and cylindrical, from wingless Red Bull cans
Rise up Phoenix, fly like Pegasus
strapped carrying scars, shell-shocked
spit on mics, lyrics of hope to fix
and rise and lift
The strong in broken places
Perform outspoken word to ovations.

Housing Hate Inflames

No Irish, No Blacks, No Dogs, No Myth
Watch the curtains twitch
Knock at the door rat a tat tat
Look at its vacant sign to attract
Sigh, and receive the breath
a circle of spit the gift
a door slammed squarely
rectangular in your face,
We won't accommodate
This is not your place

De facto dealings discriminate
In ticked off housing lists
Racial applications make Rachman rackets,
Socially engineered in clearances,
while slum landlords violate,
rental agreements and tenancy laws
Caught at the doorstep once more, waiting
Seeking shelter from 'race relations'
and policies of immigration

They burn us in plastic clad towers
Artificial facades of artifice
Made to gleam for the benefit
of the gentrified
who hide but will not seek

Songs of Grime

George Herbert and William Blake sang poems in drawing
rooms
Now we spit lyrics of innocence and experience in inner-
city bedsits
with DIY mixing equipment spinning the helms, turning the
tables
in pirate radio ships stationed
on the top of tower blocks
From the galop and Viennese Waltz to the dubstep and
skank

In ancient Greece winning poets were crowned with
wreaths
Laurels and foolhardy grime MCs battle over plinths
for block supremacy and postcode stakes
Stone Island statues dressed with Fred Perry
Roadman Supreme on the North Face
Greensleeves sampled whilst the green leaves sacred to
Apollo
Gods of Poetry go toe to toe
A Rocky Horrorshow of mercing and shanking

Akala translates Shakespeare sonnets into ghetto phonics
A Merchant of Vengeance
Putting penance and microphone to paper
Stair-welled screw-faced revenge
Measure for Measure
Opening caskets of lexical treasure
Melodious poems of praise, elegiac mourning and memory.

The Schoolboy Trap

Schoolboys trapped in William Blake House
Suspended in disbelief by a racist system
Black and brown boys fallen victims
Spit lyrical cynicism on the blocks
That they can't start from let alone sprint
Singing trap tunes in concrete prisms

III

War

War Crimes

Engrave our names, erased from monuments
Left flagging, left half-mast, outcasts
Caste out from cenotaphs, we lie in Aden
Cemeteries positioned outside in obscure theatres
to kill each other, black brother against
black brother, Black African against Askari

Salute undecorated slaves who were not named
History's X'd servicemen and women, left
to crumble, bereft under cemented empty tombs
raided long ago and still now of gratitude,
who lie deserted by campaigns of erasure,
Lascars, African Seedie Boys and Kroomen, left out
of heroic stories, whilst White British and Dominion
sailors are elevated in stone cold commemoration

Wreaths are laid at monoliths, lifting up
national myths, keeping us down, trodden
forgotten obsolete to obelisks made in concrete
Chiselled jaws of hollow marble men
who gnaw, at the marrow of our recognition
        Lest we forget them, never,
                From our monumental memory.

Union straitJacket

Successive generations are questioned
at the biometric gates, irises are scanned
Welcome To Fortress Britannia. A land
with customs to excise foreign growths
Xenophobic policing of borders,
We lock up the sons and daughters

Tebbit's cricket whites test us
Yet Stormzy rises Phoenix up above it
Our bullet proof invested second generation
Lambasted for a lack of gratitude,
burst out of a *union* strait*jacket*
The national fabric is challenged

Liberal overplay of loyalties,
lock in immigrants back to future
in a time-machine to Orwellian '84
where dissent is not a gift, we fight
wronged, for universal rights.

Empire 'Free'style

And then, there was no Empire
except the empire built in my
mind. The Empire that continues
quietly in the microagressions,
in the frowns and distanced looks
I'm given Or at least that's what
They said when slavery was abolished,
when manumission granted, when we
blacks were given votes, the crumbs
at the table, the crumpled cross
Malcolm 'X'd, in blood on the
blotted ballot paper, when we were
ushered to the front seat of the buses,
land, language and family stolen, given
social housing, put in ghettos, given
'benefits', taught the history of victors
To the extent that we doubted our own
pre-colonial agency; no longer stooping,
stopping and searching ourselves'
or bowing doffing hats and caps
to Massa, caught in our own tracks
of imagination, not racial but post-
racial denial still advancing the same
agenda in different ways. After the 13th
Amendment for the 400th time
chain ganged to the land, imprisoned
and enslaved in new forms of Empire
in new forms of chains incarcerated
iron and in plastic electronically
tagged, shackled in manacles
for wearing locks, for wearing

hoodies, shot down shopping for skittles
and iced tea trying to breathe
in the deoxygenated Empire state
of estrangement.

Another World's War

Not inscribed on your monuments
we, a part of your make   shift arrangements
Carved to fit neatly into your plans for war
Neville, you are our fair weathered supporter
We, the victims of Kitchener's propaganda prisoners

Calculated as necessary for vainglorious
victorious objectives   in another war
You rule our colonies and dominions iron rodded
Give us hot leaden shot instead
when we ask for bread, in communion we get crumbs
under the colonial master's table upon the dais of shame
Barefoot men and women given unkept promises
in world wars of losses

In irony imperialist powers redivide our territory
We   your cannon fodder
Will not swallow this for a moment longer we shape shift
like Anansi, decolonised minds that disarm
in refusal to defend your illegitimate gotten gains

Our place at the crucible of war games
does not rest   upon our ancestors
fighting for your cause, just as Orwell's Britishness
is not contested in mainstreamed rejection
Norman Tebbit's cricket whites, test us

Yet, Stormzy gets lambasted, for a lack of gratitude
Under fire water in a bullet proof in-vested
he bursts out of a Union strait Jacket,
a challenge to the national fabric

Liberal overplaying loyalties, lock in immigrant
Generating dystopic world views, dissent as a gift
endowed on the lowly visitors away from home
told it is a universal right

Shibboleths that leave their blemishes reddened raw
Oppressed, centuries of brute force, another world's war.

Copy and Paste

Ctrl C what you did to us?
Ctrl V signs to your Empire
The chains may cling and rust,
still bite in grip, but
on keyboards we are weary warriors no more

We will copy and paste our stories
Our yellow BLM lettering in capital ink
Across plaza, painted by Gaza stripped civilians
In Whitewashingtown DC high on Capitol Hill
Across nation, diaspora and dystopia,
Strong in the most broken of places
Our narratives of survival speak louder

We will sound our abeng horns
Our warning signals, heed our voice
Do not dismiss our narratives
Ctrl C and Crtl V, there is no choice
Control and conquer victorious

Chant Down Marble Men

The languages that we sung
The jokes that we played
Remember them, our ancestors

Pan-African, from Kamau to Atukwei
Okai to Braithwaite beyond the grave,
laugh in praise
and save them at the altar of memory
continuing endless conversation
generating to generation

Carry genetic memory
in your tongue's DNA
twisting helix, lick your lips
salivate and taste it, save it from
the gaze of abstract men of marble
who constrict and garble,
their reach, in staccato,
stumble trip on our un-metric,
yet the distances we cover
our own measures of achievement

Reduced measurement of our treasure
They trundle behind reinvented wheels
In the dead chests and coffins lie iambs
Silently embalmed, jarred and jammed, en-
jambed men rest in referenced reverence
at footnotes hewn in stone,
at the end of tablet and faded yellow pages

We will still breathe our hope
Structured in pidgin hybrid speech
possibilities outreach occupants who cower
grasp and grip, outwit the marble men
breathe life with ancestral power.

(Un)Reachable Moments

I

In a cuckoo flat deep in the south
He pops out, found, pulled in a social services tug
o' war, a fourteen-year-old boy
He wants to call the Samaritans
But he is lost at the other side of the crossroads
Taken back home at the end of the shift

Three months later, he pedals softly on a BMX
along a Leyton road, he's mowed down
by a silver blade, a life cut short, rammed
and knocked off by a stolen Mercedes, stabbed
repeatedly, seven seconds expire
hypovolemic shock

Crisp white shirt, blue and yellow striped tie
Done up in a morning ritual, he jokes with mum
below a well preened flat topping a lovable smile
Top sets for English, Maths and Science
What went wrong?

Plans to travel the world, dismantling bikes
then putting them back, oily jigsaw pieces
bringing joy, taken away on what he loved

Amidst the sea of floral tributes, an eyewitness
states in welled eyes that he was remarkable, boy,
a young man who'd shop, buy hats and scarves
in Primark, dish them out to the homeless
to warm them from the wintry cold

II

His cries for help are denied by browbeaten services
working in bi-polar extremes, miscommunication, missed
opportunities, hard to reach through a digital tape
emails, legal documents warrant the drowning leviathan

A child exploitation specialist can't answer the call
Still in custody, the line is dead, lost in pandemic tides
swamped in bureaucracy, beacons and lighthouses dimmed
He asks for a book and talks to the boys in blue

No big neon sign, but there is hope in the quiet times
The late-night cups of tea, outpouring vulnerability
Interventions of just doing something nice

Showing something else exists, firewalls between
kids and police, an ice cream at the seaside
toes dip in the sand, walking side by side

III

Machine gun tut-tuts of despair, disdain for youth
on dusky pavement blocks, whilst across in Italy
you'd stroll casually, a trusted passenger in *passeggiata*
you'll be welcomed to sit, have a meal or a drink
Here space is left at the table of lazy judgement,
stereo typed faces, pre-set in screw faces, erased
Squashed in a pigeon-holed box, pre-made and fabricated
Lackadaisical assumptions made in courts of law,
flimsy evidence and assertions go before untested
abruptly end in sentences

Feral youth run wild from a society lacking safe spaces
They seek the safety to explore and play in
Instead, they lay in concrete traps, entangled in gangs
without subs, on a stone island without membership
badges,
A friend asks a favour, someone has a hold on you
without you even knowing   what is happening?
Repercussions felt wet when youngers are caught
Consequences left unacknowledged by professions
In positions to help, they cry out

Our modern victims, sufferers of modern slavery await
grooming for county lines, for a moment he steps off
the trained thought, wraps, cash- strapped, burner phone
in hand, youngers and younger their single tickets expire
Left on the wrong side of the tracks, he pushes
jabs at the metallic square button, the electronic
doors of no return heave, sigh open and close.

IV

Peace

Crusades

When you encounter my culture
Day to day
You will not be threatened by the way
I
Pray,
Or what I eat or
How I say
Salaam alaikum

Neighbour,
Our God in fact may be the same
If we look a little deeper
In the face of fundamentalisms and racisms
Unorthodox schisms
That leads brothers and sisters astray

My speech and dress style will no longer perplex
Hijab or yarmulke, biretta or zucchettos
won't be of interest
Mundane differences will not divert or vex
We are the same in the most important ways
We both want peace and prosperity
Our blood flows free and evenly

In hurt and pain
Our tears of joy will taste the same
Let hate and negativity be erased,

Shake hands Christian, Jewish and Muslim crusaders
Pray for each other
For a firmer future
Terror change to terra firma
Embrace complexity
Behind the veil hides unity.

Ordinary Hybrid Bliss

Amidst maisonette curtained streets
Flanking the park in NW6
Chewing on mundane realities
Rice, peas, roast beef and chapattis
White Teeth chatter convivially
In this corner of the metropolis
Ordinary hybrid bliss

Racial difference reduced to oblivion

Concrete sciences set in mind stone
Discriminating simplification
Histories, objects, places and times
Mutants, foreigners, roles assigned
Classed as confusing, destructive objects
Fabricated into fictional reality

In the Houses of Khan and Adebisi
Two up two down
Imaginative geography vanishes
Jamaican-Yoruba-Pakistani neighbours
Everyday mundane relations
Upstairs Downstairs Hybrid Nation
Wed in the matrimony of exotic estrangement
White Teeth chatter convivially
In this corner of the metropolis
Ordinary hybrid bliss

Racial difference reduced to oblivion

We design in our mind's eye
Familiar spaces: yours and mine; ours and theirs
Arbitrary designs, (un)familiar places
Imaginative geographies, boundaries established in minds
Our land/ barbarian land binaries
Territory and mentality demarcated negative identities
Yousef and Ibrahim stutter through Bismillah
Winsome and Habiba discuss diets of how to get thinner
White Teeth chatter convivially
In this corner of the metropolis
Ordinary hybrid bliss

Racial difference reduced to oblivion

The poetics of space
Intimacies, secrecy and security
Corners, corridors, cellar rooms
Objective space reduced to imaginative value
Emotional areas made rational
By poetic process, vacant anonymous reaches
Distance converted into meaning

Oluwale and Irshad bemoan their sons'
poor performance at madrassa
White Teeth chatter convivially
In this corner of the metropolis
Ordinary hybrid bliss

Racial difference reduced to oblivion

Imaginative geography and history
Intensifying sense of self
Dramatizing distance and difference
by what is close and far away
Represents, animates, creates
otherwise silent and dangerous space
Beyond familiar boundaries

Ibrahim and Yousef listen to beats
of spontaneous and ordinary hybridity
plugged into their headphones
from their air pods lifted
Technologically trebled and based in this city
White Teeth chatter convivially
In this corner of the metropolis
Ordinary hybrid bliss

Racial difference reduced to oblivion

Intersectional identities, solidarity
Class, gender, sex and faith
rendering race unthinkable
Beyond skin invisible

White Teeth chatter convivially
In this corner of the metropolis
Ordinary hybrid bliss
Racial difference reduced to oblivion.

Smethwick Melts

In the Blackest of Countries
Smethwick smelters swelter, forging futures
uncertain under the welding torch, 360 degree heat
Industrial revolutions, movement
Empire striking back, blacksmiths on metal, vexed
Hammer and tongs on anvils
Culmination of a history, triangulated trade
Enslavement, steely colour bars, colonisation,
Low respect and wages, war, welcome
to the most racist of places
where rivers run blood

Metal foundries, industrial complexes
Founded by fathers Boulton & Watt
in the seventeen sixties
Smethwick Engine powering,
wheel of industry
Hardening steel structures of slavery
Steel frameworks making brilliant exhibitions
in polished Crystal Palaces
Railing rolling stock manufacturing
Steel screws fastening Hope
& Sons steel window systems and gearings
Steel pen nibs for British Pens
writing immigrant destiny

Metal casts aside cheap colonial labour
To fill, the avoided, Asian and Black neighbours
In the nineteen fifties Midlands car boom
Soon the signs read 'No dogs, Blacks or Asians'
Samaritans cross pavements in gloom

Smethwick surrenders to racism
If you want a nigger neighbour vote Labour
The slogan legitimates hate, officially
on the ballot paper
The racist tail of the parliamentary dog wags,
licking its lips at a bone of contention
at the '64 General Election
Fearful of losing votes and deep seats
of hostility, blue and red have no room
for Blacks and Asians
and accommodate themselves to prejudice

Peter Griffiths stands at the parliamentary platform
On his whistle stop tour
Station managing mouthpiece, puppeteer
Manipulating, pulling population's heartstrings of popular
fear
Commander, mobilising racist working-class sentiment,
A fight to end immigration, calling to arms,
repatriation of 'the coloureds', send them packing
Back to the Colonies,
The irony! Brought to provide favours
for post-war shortages of labour

Labour wins the election
Yet Griffiths gets Smethwick,
an electoral return favoured
for the crucifixion of immigrants
Finder of the holy grail:
Undermining working class support for Labour
Exploiter of those housing anxiety over shortages
Blaming Asians and Blacks
A cynical electoral stratagem
that got him elected, a pat on the back again

He who wrote the toxic tome *A Question of Colour?*
Poison penning lessons from Apartheid
In solidarity with the beleaguered population,
Malcolm X came to Smethwick, press took his picture
at Marshall Street, where some residents filed petitions
with Griffiths, arranging for Council authority
to keep the street white,
while Asian customers waited for hours
at barbers cutting sharp racial divisions,
refused drinks at the Ivy Bush, colour Bar

Where other residents received race hate
material fabricated from National Socialists,
Vigilante Leagues and Keep Britain White
Malcolm warned of another Holocaust,
treatment as Jews under Hitler,
preventing fascists from erecting gas ovens

Now the Ivy Bush serves curries,
the British favourite dish,
six nights a week
a multicultural pub, smelting the good
mixing melting pot of cultures
Morrisseys, Mahmoods, Middletons,
Singhs, Dixons and Akhtars neighbours,
Exchange sugar bowls sweetening tensions
Post-industrial foundry towns
of the lost and found,
Forging ahead iron allegiances
based on the mettle of humanity,
An alchemy of hope.

Fly a New Flag

For the flags of the Ashanti and St. George, may you flutter gracefully

Fly my kente, fly my union jack
Flutter between boxes, tick heritage white and black
In symmetry, escape the pinning of your wings

Above the ignorance, climb and vault your horse
Knights high on hybrid influence, somersault with voice
Pink sword creole tongues extract Excalibur's auction block

Enter the circus tent of clowns, the medieval joust
Knock off opponents from their lofty pedestalled mounts
Fill lances stormy blue with ink and watch the mighty fall

Saunter through their hall of mirrors, without a doubt
Distorting visions recalibrate, eyes open wide now
Righting myopic wrongs and rights blinkering both sides

Fly my kente, fly my union jack
Trussed in chainmail and helmets: tam o'shanters, rasta caps
Flash your locks, break open rusty chains and manacles
Bobo Shanti turbans corkscrew glass ceiling capitals

Fly high my brethren over chequered citadels
Gallop the show jumping poles of prejudice
Burn Massa's sugar cane crop whips, emancipate
burning stalks of *cannes brûlées* high above your heads

Fly away one nation builders, with your mythical moats and walls
Drop the ballast of urban planners who constrict our worlds

Who construct us in serpentine twists and turns

Spurned by history's forked medieval tongues touch lips
Fly above high-rise township tower blocks, the ghetto
labyrinths
Crush plastic clad projections, augmented walkways in the
sky
Ethnics out of sight and mind, cleansed and gentrified

Fly my kente, fly my union jack
Reach Zion, reach the promised land,
Sit for a first meal and feast in commensality
There is no turning back

Knights together round a table, of inclusivity.

Acknowledgements

Grateful acknowledgment is made to the editors and staff of the following book anthologies, magazines and websites, in which versions of these poems originally appeared: *dyst Literary Journal, Poor Yorick Literary Journal, Scissortail Quarterly, Rigorous, Sundress Publications* and *Writers Workshop India.*

'Wake Up Call' appeared in *dyst* Literary Journal Issue 5, 31 March 2021, RoseyRavelston Books

'Melanin Masked White' featured in Poor Yorick Literary Journal, Special Issue: Masks, April 2021

'Misread' appeared in Scissortail Quarterly, Issue 2, Scissortail Press, March 2021

'Nyankopoxyican Breath of Fresh Air' appeared in Rigorous, Volume 5, Issue 2, June 2021, featured in the Nombono Anthology - Speculative Poetry by BIPOC poets, Sundress Publications, edited by Akua Lezli Hope, October 27, 2021. The poem received a nomination for the Best Long Form Poem category and was included in the 2022 Rhysling Anthology, selected by the Science Fiction & Fantasy Poetry Association, ed F.J Bergmann & Brian U. Garrison, February 2022. 'Nyankopoxyican Breath of Fresh Air' will be published in 'The Year's Best African Speculative Fiction (2022), Volume Two, ed Oghenechovwe Donald Ekpeki, Eugen Bacon & Milton Davis'

'Crusades' and 'Ordinary Hybrid Bliss' appeared in Beyond Alienation, Hatred and Terror: Compatriots with Love and Living-Kind (An Anthology of Poems), Authorspress, edited by Meera Chakravorty, Marcus Bussey, Camila Mozzini-Alister and Ananta Kumar Giri, January 23, 2022; Poetry in Times of Conflict series, Writers Workshop India, to be released this year.